Becoming a Little League Mom

A Mom's Guide to Little League Baseball

by

Deborah C. Alderink

DORRANCE PUBLISHING CO., INC.
PITTSBURGH, PENNSYLVANIA 15222

To my husband, David, the best little league dad and coach. To my sons, Travis and Kiel, my little league all-stars. And to all my family and friends who contributed to this book.

The contents of this work, including, but not limited to, the accuracy of events, people, and places depicted; opinions expressed; permission to use previously published materials included; and any advice given or actions advocated are solely the responsibility of the author, who assumes all liability for said work and indemnifies the publisher against any claims stemming from publication of the work.

The author wishes to clarify that the term "little league," which appears throughout her book, is meant to be a general definition for little boys' baseball and does not necessarily represent any views or representations of the official Little League ® organization.

ISBN: 978-1-4349-0346-4
Printed in the United States of America

First Printing

For more information or to order additional books, please contact:
Dorrance Publishing Co., Inc.
701 Smithfield Street
Pittsburgh, Pennsylvania 15222
U.S.A.
1-800-788-7654
www.dorrancebookstore.com

Introduction

No one really prepares a mom for the time of her life when little league baseball is all that matters. Certainly, she receives nothing like the gentle, gradual preparation offered when she became a mom for the first time. Remember those hospital-sponsored, mandated childbirth classes where nurses tried to prepare you methodically for the most devastating pain and biological disturbances you ever would experience? You learn after just one class you really would prefer to not attend a second, but you know you should prepare yourself as much as possible for delivering your soon-to-be little league baseball player.

Little league baseball is very similar to having a baby, except there are no classes. Actually, little information, other than word of mouth, exists for the soon-to-be mom of a little league baseball all-star. Most often, mothers are forced to rely on other moms' stories, which usually include bragging about their all-star little leaguer or horror stories about ill-adjusted players who cannot function in today's society without a carefully balanced drug and counseling program.

It's no wonder that moms entering the fast-paced, ritualistic arena of little league baseball are ill-prepared. Take me for example: At first I found myself relying on my fight-or-flight instinct simply to survive. After I became acclimatized, I learned the ropes and became one of them.

Yes, it is true.

I can admit it now.

I am a Little League Mom.

We Little League Moms are easily recognized. We drive vans or station wagons full of kids (and sometimes animals) wearing baseball hats, swinging bats, popping a ball into a glove, spitting, and scratching. The windows of the vehicles are painted with a mixture of fingerprints, nose prints, and drool from big-wad bubble gum. There even may be a chip in the windshield from a fugitive hard ball when we parked too close to home plate. We tote coolers of water, six packs of electrolyte drinks, ice packs and first aid kits. We run frantically to the ball diamond, trying to make it before the singing of the national anthem, with a glove someone forgot. We keep sewing baskets in our trunks, equipped with huge needles to lace gloves. We carry pant strings, stirrups, and good luck charms in our purses or pockets. We have either cameras choking our necks or poor posture from backpacks full of video equipment and toddlers squirming to get free from our arms. We can be seen frequently near or in the dugout, coaxing little brothers or sisters out of harm's way. We are found wandering the concession stands, portable johns, or parking lots searching for straying children, sometimes using the public announcement system as a last resort. And every once in a while, when permitted, we run onto the field to give first aid to an injured player.

An introduction to little league baseball is presented in this book, as well as recommendations for gaining some control of most situations in this hectic, yet amazing, world. Also included is information on signing up your little leaguer; the playing field and the object of the game; what the players do; who are the "baseball cops;" acceptable and not-so-acceptable (but tolerable) behavior; the language of baseball; bleacher personalities; outfitting your all-star; what moms should wear; cheering etiquette; what to do when the coach won't put your baby in the game; responsibilities of the coach's wife; the all-star game; and what to expect from the grand finale.

As a veteran Little League Mom, I wish you and your little leaguers great success. Remember, as you are scrubbing grass and mud stains out of those white pants over and over again, trying to pick the melted chewing gum out of your shoes, sporting a nice sunburn on only your knees and nose, and discovering the most effective anti-itch cream—it's a wonderful time of your life. Have fun!

Chapter One
Sign-Ups

The little league process begins when your player signs up with the local association. It is important that your future little leaguer show at least some interest in the sport of baseball. There will be clues: maybe you noticed your player hitting a ball off a tee-stick or playing ball with friends in the yard. These are good signs. Even collecting baseball cards or routinely wearing a baseball cap can be signs that you have a true little league baseball player. Hitting dogs, siblings, or other children with sticks, a ball, or even a bat can be signs—but those children may be better suited for football or hockey.

It's also a good idea that you, the little league Mom, sign up in person. The first step in avoiding a disastrous season is to make sure you know the days and times to enlist. Missing the designated sign-up times can create an impression you are flighty or cause havoc for the league organizers. Even worse, you may be placed on a waiting list. It's a kind of purgatory between the hell of waiting for a call to be placed on a team ("Did they call mom? Did they? Everyone else is on a team but me!") and the heaven of your child being a contributing player.

When you arrive at the designated registration, place, be prepared for noise. You'll see dads in groups of three discussing past, present, and future hopeful all-star players; moms in a hurry; and of course baseball players, all anxiously waiting for their shot at league stardom. Perhaps you enter during a rare quiet time, when all the coaches stop talking and watch you and your all-star slowly approach the sign-up table, all the while sizing up your child—and maybe even you. You'll be tempted to pull your shirt down over your hips.

There will be some sort of paperwork requiring accurate information, including a "hold harmless agreement" in fine print. You will have to sign a statement saying the league is not responsible for anything untoward that may happen to your all-star. It's important to realize that there is a risk of injury with base sliding, swinging bats, and out-of-sight fly balls.

It's a well-known fact that most dads never can seem to remember the exact birth year of their child. Keep in mind, any misinformation can endanger your player of being assigned to the wrong age group. Your child could end up with a uniform that could be used as a tarp to protect the field in foul weather, or one so tight that it could impede circulation to important parts of the body.

If there is a spot on the registration card for "team requested," then it may help to find out who is coaching each team. Frequently, veteran coaches attend the sign-ups to make sure they recruit seasoned, talented players or to avoid others who are not so talented. Discreetly size-up these coaches. Don't be misled by their physical attributes; baldness, large abdominal girth, and scratching in moist crevices seem the accepted norm in little league baseball. Remember, it is a "man's sport," so grunting, farting, spitting, scratching, adjusting body parts, and chewing are all part of the experience. It's the coaches' mannerisms that should assist in your final selection, if you are allowed one at all. If you want simply to ease into the little league process, try to avoid the coach who is pacing, chewing, and rocking back and forth while biting his nails and spitting them onto the sign-up table. If you are someone who likes a more direct approach, look for the loud talker with robust laughter. During a close game, however, you can expect a lot of yelling, explicit gestures, and arguing with the umpire. There is always the soft-spoken coach who can't establish eye contact with you and who is convinced that everyone is an all-star. He could be the right choice for you—just don't expect a winning season.

Sometimes it's important for you to sign up at the same time as your player. You might have to participate in the fund-raisers or work in the concession stand selling candy, ice cream, popsicles, or drinks to hundreds of kids less than ten years old. You may be assigned to repairing uniforms or assisting as a base coach. You should volunteer for highly visible positions such as concession stands or picnics. Everyone in your community will take note of those moms who don't sign up. Non-volunteers are treated with distaste for a long time to come, and you will have no privileges or voice in any league business. Do your share, and put pressure on the moms who aren't doing their share.

Finally, make sure your check doesn't bounce. If you are branded for insufficient funds when paying for a little league registration fee, it will be a topic of discussion at every sporting event, forever!

Chapter Two
The Playing Field

Every park where baseball is played has a ball diamond of dirt or grass. There may be a fence with a backstop behind the home plate for the protection of spectators and to assist the catcher in getting a loose ball. It's very important that if you choose to sit behind home plate, then you must pay close attention to the game at all times. You must have quick reflexes to dodge flying objects.

In the center of the diamond is a hill of dirt called the "mound." The mound should be a distance of 46 feet from the home plate. (It is not unusual that a dad of a pitcher actually measures this distance.) In the center of the mound is a rubber mat, sometimes so worn that all you will notice is a shred of one that used to be there. The mound is where the pitcher stands while throwing the ball. When the pitcher "toes the rubber," that means he or she is setting up on the mound. The pitcher must have one foot on the plate while pitching to the batter. Sometimes in little league, a dad or a machine pitches the ball.

Around the diamond are three bases and a home plate. Bases are also sometimes called "bags" or "sacks." Home plate sometimes is called "dish." Chalk lines connect the four bases. (You always can find the volunteer dad who operates the chalk machine on a windy day because he's covered in white dust and spits more than usual.) Hopefully the volunteer dad who marks the field is sober so the lines are straight. These bases are sixty feet apart and, along with the home plate, they form the diamond, which is the "infield." Around the diamond is a grassy or dirt field called the "outfield." The outfield then is divided up into the right field, left center field, right center field, and left field. The "alley" is the section of the outfield between the outfielders, also known as the "gap." (No – not the brand-named store, but that's how you may remember it.)

The "batter circle" is the area beside home plate where the batter must stand while at bat. Most often, little leaguers in the batter's box look to the bleachers to signal to their parents that they want more gum. The batter cannot leave this position after the pitcher comes to the set position or begins the windup. The "catcher's box" is the area behind home plate where the catcher must remain until the pitcher delivers the ball. There usually is a chalked area in the shape of a circle for the "on deck," or the batter-in-waiting, to stand, swing the bat, size up the pitcher, and warm up for the next at bat. It is not a good idea to place a port-a-potty close to the on deck spot because it becomes a suggestion to go potty. Your little batter forgets they are up next to bat, and they choose to use the bathroom. Everyone will begin to look for the little leaguer, sometimes resorting to a public announcement. You, the Little League Mom, will be blamed for your little leaguer's lack of bladder control!

The "bull pen," which is beyond the outfield fence, is where the pitcher warms up with someone who can catch the ball. The starting pitcher, after warming up, will take the mound while a relief pitcher goes into the bull pen to warm up in case he or she is selected to pitch. Never approach your pitcher as he or she is warming up in the bull pen. Never!

"Fair territory" is part of the playing field within and including the first base and third base lines. It extends from home plate to the bottom of the playing field fence.

"Foul lines" are lines extending from home plate through first and third bases to the outfield. A "foul ball" is one that goes beyond these lines; a foul ball allows the batter to bat another ball.

"Foul territory" is part of the playing field outside the first and third base lines that extends to the fence.

The "strike zone" is the imaginary, most often highly disputable, area over home plate between the batter's armpits and knees when the batter is positioned to swing. Any pitch delivered through this area is called a strike (by most seeing eye dogs, anyway). This area is always the center of controversy between parents—especially of pitchers—and the umpire.

There are two "dugouts" where players (including starters and relief players) sit. Dugouts are usually lower than the bleacher area, but in many fields, they can be a bench which is fenced-in. A lot of activity occurs in a dugout—sitting is rare. Little League Moms are rarely, if ever, allowed in the dugout unless your little leaguer gives you a look or a motion indicating they want a drink or something to chew and spit. It's important to maintain your distance, as this is a bonding space for players and their coaches.

Now that you know and understand the field components, make sure you can locate the exact field where the game will be played. Sometimes there are several fields in a sports complex. Also, be sure that you know the name of your team. If you forget, at least know the color of the uniform and matching hat. It distracts players and spectators when a Little League Mom wanders aimlessly from field to field, looking for her player. Never wave to your player when you finally find the right field. Never stop a game to ask an outfielder—or worse, the umpire—for directions. Even though you have no clue where you are going, don't admit it.

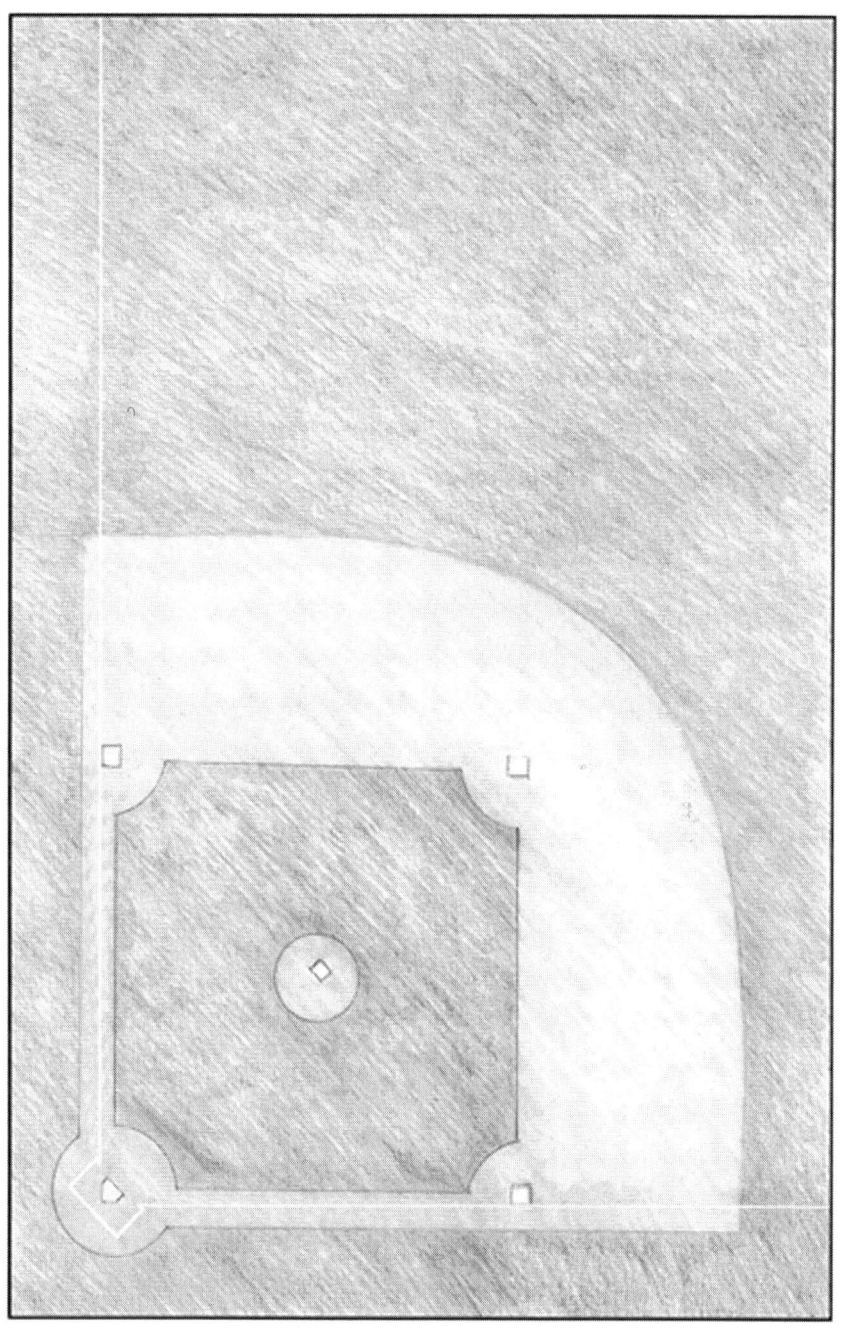

Chapter Three
The Object of the Game

The object of the game is to hit the pitched ball, or the ball perched on a rubber "tee" (which looks like a stick on a rubber base), get on base, move around the diamond, and eventually cross home plate for a run. Whoever has the most runs at the end of four innings (the usual game length in tee-ball little league) wins.

It is important to understand that little league beginners really don't know if they win or lose. It is so common to hear a little leaguer, after suffering a staggering loss, say, "We creamed them," then smile and go off to get ice cream or soda pop. They don't care. The parents, however, seem to care a little too much most of the time. Some leagues actually have discussed not keeping score so as not to offend or disrupt the normal development of their players. But baseball is all about keeping score. Nothing is more exciting than watching a little leaguer cross home plate, slap high-fives with teammates who have all lined up between home plate and the dugout, and then check the run count on the scoreboard.

Most leagues have a five-run rule, which means once a team scores five runs in any inning, no matter how many outs, the next team gets to bat. This five-run rule helps keep the game on time. It also helps dilute any devastation for the not-so-talented team.

Speaking of rules, the rules pertaining to the field where the game is played are called "ground rules." Coaches and umpires have a copy of these rules with them at all times. It's their Bible. Sections are tabbed for easy reference. Any controversy, and out comes the rule book. Moms rarely care about these rules, unless, of course, she is married to the rule book carrier, or the rule causes emotional scars to her little leaguer.

Chapter Four
The Players and the Plays They (are supposed to) Make

There are ten defensive players on the field. A "baseman" is someone who is responsible to defend the base (apparently this name was assigned prior to the women's liberation movement.) The infield consists of three basepersons (first, second, and third), a shortstop, a catcher, and a pitcher. The name "shortstop" has nothing to do with the height of the player. The shortstop covers the space between the second and third base, and sometimes the outfield, too.

The infielders can also be known as the "cut-off men." This doesn't mean guys with crew cuts or players without all of their appendages. A cut-off man is a fielder who intercepts a ball being thrown in, usually from the outfield. Coaches are located near first and third base. A pitcher stands on a mound in the center of the infield. The catcher squats in front of an umpire, behind home plate in the catcher's box.

The first baseman has to be quick and attentive, as most of the play occurs at this base. Typically there are two bases, or bags, at this position so the runner can overrun, or run past, the first base. The double bag is a safety bag. The white bag is for the fielder to step on, and the orange bag is for the runner. The system usually works well, but new little leaguers easily can get confused, and a collision is not out of the question, especially if the first baseman also plays football and tries to block the base. Once the player turns the corner and takes his or her foot off the base after the pitcher has the ball back, they are fair game for a "pick-off tag." In other words, the pitcher can throw the ball to the first baseman, and if the runner does not have at least one appendage (actually any body part, including a nose) on the plate, the runner can be tagged out. Little leaguers typically cry when they are tagged out. The actual tag should be a light tap—sometimes, however, it's a sock, a push, or a punch, and then the dads get involved. Don't get involved. The situation tends to resolve itself quickly.

The second baseman at least should have the ability to catch a fly ball. This position actually covers the space between first base and the shortstop. The third baseman must have a good, strong, accurate throwing arm because he or she must throw the ball all the way across the field to first base or to the pitcher, maybe even to home base. The third baseman also must have a strong sense of the game to know when the ball, closely traveling along the outer marker or line, is a foul ball or a line drive.

The catcher has to squat throughout the whole game, so good knees are a must. In tee-ball, the catcher simply stands in a box next to the batter and is responsible for catching the ball, or picking it up, when another player throws it into the catcher's position. It's also very important, Mom, that the catcher wears underwear, for squatting in front of a crowd while wearing tight-fitting, white pants. As a mom, you can't help but notice stains or cleavage if present. It's just natural.

Nerves of steel and the ability to handle pain are more traits of a good catcher; he or she squats in front of the umpire and is responsible for keeping the ball from hitting the umpire. It's also usually a good idea for the catcher to be a "scrapper" Who can chatter things that distract, upset, disturb, or incite fights with the batter. Hassling the batter by saying things typically not flattering and generally untrue actually is the best part of being a catcher.

Catchers are the "gate keepers"; a catcher has to be ready to tag a runner stealing home base. If the catcher has the ball, he or she must not allow runners to cross the plate. Catchers get pushed, shoved, clobbered, and stomped on. They take a while, sometimes, to stand up straight. The best catchers also are football players or hockey players—"no fear" types of people. So, Mom, that means you have to be, too—you can't gasp loudly.

Catchers have to be able to suit up in the catcher's gear, which includes the face guard, helmet, chest protector, and leg protectors. When you see the gear for the first time, it is not uncommon to become fearful. It's an important position and can be exciting. Catchers spring up to get a fly ball, chase a ball down before it touches the backstop, and can catch a fly ball that is hit straight up into the sky. They rip off their faceguards to look for overthrown balls. Their gear prepares and protects them for play.

Another important function of the catcher is to call the pitch for the pitcher. The catcher places a finger down an inner thigh to call a fast ball or a curve. After the catcher calls the pitch, the pitcher either nods in agreement or shakes his or her head in disagreement. This signals the catcher to call the pitch the pitcher wants. When the pitcher agrees to a pitch, the catcher re-positions behind home plate, awaiting the toss. This doesn't happen until the players get a little older. When they put the middle finger out—no good comes out of it.

The pitcher must have a strong arm with some throwing control. He or she must wind up, using the body, especially the legs, and throw the ball 46 feet to the batter's box. Pitchers are called "hurlers" sometimes. The pitcher is the "lighthouse." He or she moves all around the mound, surveying the field, studying the batter, and maintaining eye contact with the coaches, while keeping one foot on the rubber. Pitchers usually have a special glove, which costs a lot and takes a long time to soften up. Once they throw the ball, they must cover home plate or first base. They wear their hats low or to the side, look mean, growl and hiss to intimidate the batter, spit, chew, and grab their body parts. It's all part of being a pitcher.

A left-handed pitcher is referred to as a "southpaw." Years ago, this term came about because a left-handed pitcher's throwing arm faced south at Wrigley Field. Left-handed pitchers are highly desirable.

The starting pitcher begins the game and usually throws for only four innings. If this pitcher is really good, then he or she is called an "ace." The relief pitcher replaces the starting pitcher. Finally, there may be a closing pitcher, or "closer," as years in baseball progress. This is a pitcher who comes in for the last inning or two to close the game.

The outfield consists of the right fielder, left center fielder, right center fielder, and left fielder. The outfielders move about the distant land, patrolling for a flying baseball. They get lucky now and then and get to catch a fly ball or chase a grounder. Outfielders should have a fairly strong, accurate arm to get the ball to either the cut-off man or the base before the runner for the out. Unfortunately, it is common for a weaker player to be placed in the outfield when they are young, as there is very little action. Technically they are playing, but they don't really do anything but hang out. Since there is usually little action in the outfield in the beginning, outfielders will become easily distracted. A distracted outfielder will chase butterflies, or spin, or even sit down somewhere in the territory they are supposed to be patrolling.

The "batter" is an offensive player from the opposite team. He or she approaches home plate based on a schedule, or batting order. There are always two batters: one actually doing the swinging, and another waiting in a special box to the right of home plate called the on-deck spot. This batter-in-waiting is said to be "on deck." Once the batter hits the ball, he or she is then called a "runner." A runner is an offensive player who advances toward, touches, or returns to any base.

A "switch hitter" is a player who is able to bat left-handed or right-handed. Switch hitters are a coach's secret weapon because switch hitters bat from the opposite side that the pitch is thrown.

A "clean-up hitter" is a player who hits fourth in the batting order. What is supposed to happen is that the first three batters get on a base and "load" the bases, which means that there is a runner on all three bases. The clean-up hitter then hits a line drive or home run and brings them all in for a "grand slam home run."

A "designated hitter" (abbreviated DH) is a player who bats in the pitcher's spot in the line-up. The DH does not have a fielding position.

Finally, the "clutch hitter" is a player who has proven that he or she can get a hit in stressful situations, if there is such a thing in little league baseball.

To make things even more confusing, there is something called a "utility player," who can fill in any position. A good coach rotates the players when they are young, to assess where their talents can best be served. A coach that is trying to relive his life places more talented players in the key positions, inning after inning.

When you feel you are ready, call your player by his or her position: "Hey, First Baseman!" "Hey, Catcher!" or by the player's uniform number: "That's you, Nine!" after a successful hit. You will be rewarded with the widest smile, a wink, a tip of the hat, or a recognition nod.

Chapter Five
The Baseball Cops

The rules of the league are enforced by two umpires who are usually trained and sometimes paid. The home plate umpire is easily recognized by the black and blue marks on his or her legs, thighs, and arms, though hopefully not the throat. The base umpire patrols the field, usually behind the pitcher. Most people say to qualify as a baseball official you must be blind, deaf, and dumb. Man or woman, the umpires must have nerves of solid rock. They can't wear their feelings on their sleeves, since sometimes the comments get a little personal.

Umpires must be strong and never show weakness. Fans love to boo umpires; it's just part of the game. Arguing a call is to be expected, as long as there are no weapons or threats involved, and it doesn't go on too long. Umpires make the call. They either yell their decision or make gestures. They are criticized if they don't speak loud and clear. They are criticized if they do speak loud and clear. They are criticized if they speak too low or too high.

When an umpire signals to the right of the batter, it means a "strike." (signaling can be holding up two fingers, pointing, gesturing, nodding, etc.). If your little leaguer is the pitcher, then you want strikes. If your little league player is the batter, strikes are bad. Gesturing to the left of the batter means a "ball," which is a pitch outside the strike zone. This is considered a free pass.

Four balls means the batter (and other batters who may be on base) get to advance to the next base. Some umpires grunt loudly for a strike or yell "No!" when it's a ball. An extended middle finger pointed at the audience means "Shut up." When umpires cross or wave their arms as a runner is racing to the base before a successfully thrown ball, it means the runner is safe. If the umpire puts a thumb down, and sometimes makes a bodily gesture towards the ground, it means the runner is out.

A fair ball is a ball that lands in fair ball territory. A foul ball, on the other hand, is a ball that lands in foul ball territory. Umpires are supposed to yell, "Foul ball!" really loudly. A foul is also signaled by an arm wave toward the left of the third or first baseline. If a tee-ball player hits the tee, it is considered a foul ball. Controversy will erupt if the little leaguer hits the tee, but gets enough of the ball to put it into play.

Umpires call "Balk," which is a penalty for an illegal movement by the pitcher. A balk is really bad because a base runner gets to advance a base. Everyone blames the pitcher. If you're the mother of the pitcher, try to look remorseful. Simply tell the crowd that you will punish the pitcher when you get home. That will appease them.

When an umpire throws a coach out of the game, the umpire will reach forward with his or her entire body and point to the dugout, or the locker room, or the road.

When umpires take off their gear and walk off the field, that means they have had enough, and the game is done. Umpires never walk off the field quietly.

Chapter Six
Acceptable and Not-so-acceptable, but Tolerable, Behavior

It is important to accept the mannerisms and personal hygiene of a ball player during a game. Rules of proper etiquette no longer exist once the ball player, whether a girl or a boy, walks onto the field or into the dugout. First and foremost, they spit. Spitting becomes a talent all in itself. The spit cud is called a "loogie." Players compete on the distance a loogie can go, the size of the loogie, and the total number of disgusting looks received while walking around with a slimy trail of tag-behind-loogie dripping from the corner of a lip. If little leaguers are not spitting, they are chewing huge wads of bubble gum. Somehow, one piece of gum turns into several pieces of gum. It can scare a nervous mom who may be afraid of someone choking. They also like to chew not-so-edible foods, such as sunflower seeds, just to spit the seed pod out in front of you.

Loud farting is common, especially during a critical play such as stealing a base or sliding into home plate. The coach, the umpire, the audience—they all fart. No one ever comments; everyone simply doesn't acknowledge it. However, the uniform pants are white, so hopefully the fart isn't wet. If it is, never fear; have the ballplayer scoot his or her fanny on the dirt. No one but the Little League Mom, who will wash the uniform later, will know the true identity of the stain. Gloves are always necessary for handling soiled laundry, such as grass-or dirt-stained pants.

Because the game of baseball involves a lot of running, sprinting, jumping, and stretching, body parts become displaced from their original loosely-hanging-yet-comfortable position—for boys, anyway. So, it is acceptable for boys to touch their crotches to adjust all that is tucked into baseball pants. Male baseball players also love to knock their protective cup, making a loud noise and drawing attention to themselves.

Booing, horsing around, fighting, scrapping, spitting, laughing, or challenging calls made by the officials is normal for little leaguers. They are supposed to do these things. It is so uncool to scold or correct a little leaguer who is chattering in the dugout, unless, of course, the chatter contains the "F word."

Last but not least, picking one's nose and flicking boogers will never be accepted or tolerated—for little leaguers or spectators!

Chapter Seven
Basic Baseball Language:
What's It All Mean?

B aseball has a language of its own. Terms you will hear, at least as a beginner, are detailed in this chapter. You easily can build your baseball vocabulary once you understand the basic language and you player continues through the years.

An **inning** is a segment of time in which one team gets three outs. If it's the beginning of the inning for the first team (the visiting team), then it's the "top" of the inning. The second half of the inning is called the "bottom" of the inning, when the home team is at bat.

- A **Double header** is when the same teams play two games back-to-back. One mom to another: bring food. These players are starved between games. If you are the home team mom, prepare food that is easily digestible for your players. You'll gain an advantage if you provide heavy food for the visitors, so they feel sleepy and lazy.
- **Interference** is obviously when something or someone interferes with the game. Examples are if the base runner obstructs the throwing of the ball, or if the

umpire accidentally gets in the way of a play, or if a spectator touches the ball while it's in play.

- A **Rain delay,** or rain check, occurs when a game is cancelled due to rain. Sometimes teams will play the game in drizzling rain. Any lightning, though, and the game is called, which means there will be no game that day.
- Some batting terms include:
- **Base on balls:** Also called a walk. If a pitcher throws four balls, the hitter advances to first base and you may hear, "Travis gets a base on balls."
- **Choke Up:** When a batter moves his or her hands up toward the fat end of the bat—not when a player aspirates some food.
- **Single:** When the batter hits a ball well enough to get to first base—it has nothing to do with the player's marital status.
- **Double:** When the batter hits the ball and gets to second base—it has nothing to do with future alcoholism.
- **Triple:** When the batter hits the ball and gets to third base. This is very exciting—almost as good as a home run.
- **Homerun or dinger:** When a player makes it all the way around the bases, crosses home plate and scores a run.
- **Grand slam:** Most people associate this term with a huge breakfast, but it's really a home run that is hit while there are runners on all bases, and everyone crosses home base to score four runs. This is a big deal for the hitter, and really bad for the pitcher. All the players from the dugout line up at home plate and give high-fives, screaming in victory. If you are the mother of the hitter, you must stand up and cheer loudly. If you are the mother of the pitcher, however, you have to endure your player's pain. Mothers of pitchers and grand slam hitters do not exchange eye contact.
- **Line drive:** When a ball is hit in a straight line anywhere in the fair play area.

- **Line drive out:** When the ball is hit by the batter directly into a fielder's glove.
- **Ground out:** When a ball is hit along the ground and scooped into an infielder's glove. The infielder then throws the ball to first base to get the batter out.
- **Pop up or pop fly:** When a ball is hit high into the air, and the infielder or the catcher catches it; it never hits the ground. A fly ball can be caught in the outfield.
- **Swing and a miss:** When a batter swings at a pitched ball and misses it. Sometimes it's very common to hear announcers almost sing, "Swwwwingggg and a miss!"
- **Full count:** Three balls and two strikes. The next pitch will result in either an out or a walk. Timid little leaguers will usually hold out for the easy walk on base.
- **Slide:** When the runner skids on the ground and touches the base. Sliding very rarely is attempted at first base, which is why there are two bases at that position.
- **An out:** Occurs after three strikes, a caught fly ball, or a tag off a base.
- **Touch the base or retouch the base:** When a base runner has to return to the base and touch it. Sometimes the batter, now called a base runner, runs so fast that they skip the base, jump over it, or forget to touch it. The opposing team's spectators always notice! They start screaming, "Ump, he forgot to touch the base! Then the runner's team's spectators start screaming, "Touch the base!" or "Go back!" It gets very exciting. The little leaguer stands there, bewildered.
- **Pickle or run down:** When a base runner is trapped between bases. Each infielder then throws the ball back and forth, while the runner tries to get to a base, or is tagged for an out.
- **"He's a looker" or "Caught looking":** When a batter doesn't swing while three strikes just pass by. My favorite baseball broadcaster, Ernie Harwell, the voice of the Detroit Tigers, always used to say, "Called out for excessive window shopping!"

- **Crowding the plate:** When a player moves close to the plate. It's very rarely done in little league with an inexperienced pitcher because no one wants to be smacked with a thrown ball.
- **Stealing:** When a base runner advances to the next base in between pitches.
- **Beanball:** A pitch intentionally thrown at the batter—which can start some interesting buzzing and gesturing among the spectators.
- **Bloop:** A fly ball that lands in between the infield and the outfield.
- **Bunt:** A soft hit that lands just in front of the home plate, forcing the pitcher to run forward and the catcher to run toward it, and sometimes the third baseman to run toward it as well.

Those are some of the spoken words you'll hear; the unspoken words include body or hand signals, especially between the third base coach and the batter or an on-base player. They slap their faces, legs, noses, ears, or heads, over and over. Every once in a while, some dad will brag that he knows what the signals mean. Ignore him.

Chapter Eight
Bleacher Personalities

When you arrive at your first game, you will notice a set of bleachers. Sometimes there are separate bleachers for the home team and the visiting team; sometimes there are no bleachers, just grass; sometimes there is no grass, just mud; and sometimes there are only a baseball field and a backstop fence. If you are in your own neighborhood, your player's team is the "home" team. If you have to drive a distance, your players are the "visitors" or "guests." It's important to select the appropriate set of bleachers. Cheering for the opposite team, also known as the enemy, is simply not done. If you have relatives on the opposite team, try to talk to them before the game starts; this is acceptable behavior. But do not sit with them. You must sit with your team's parents or on the invisible line between the bleachers, or cluster of lawn chairs, and the blankets.

You can't help but stare into the bleachers, examining the seating arrangements and types of people already sitting there, all moved in with their chair backs, blankets, assortment of drinks and food, umbrellas, and electronic equipment. During a little league baseball game, bleachers become a community of people consisting mostly of women, some men, grandpas, grandmas, brothers, sisters, aunts, uncles, scouts, and other community members looking for something to do on a warm summer day.

You should expect to encounter certain personalities while in the bleachers:

➤ One of the most obnoxious spectators is the "screamer." The screamer is usually a soft-spoken, short woman who reaches new levels of vocal heights during a baseball game. The screaming begins at the onset of action and intensifies logarithmically. By the end of the game, the screamer sits alone.

➤ The "backseat umpire" can be a man or a woman who never agrees with even one call the umpire makes. He or she tends to sit behind home plate; if there are no bleachers at the ball field, backseat umpires bring chairs and perch there, sometimes holding on to the backstop fencing. They say things like, "Are we in the same game?" "Clearly it caught the edge of the plate," and "Looks good to me." Because their strike zone differs with the umpire's, the true baseball cop, the backseat umpire comments on every call until he or she is ejected from the game. It's appropriate to cheer, "Get out of here!" or "Hit the road, Jack!" and boo loudly when the backseat umpire leaves the field. It is not appropriate to spit, throw mud or candy, or use weapons of any sort.

➤ "Backseat coaches" sometimes are mistaken for backseat umpires. The only difference is they lean against the dugout and try and override the coach. They offer unsolicited advice to team members from the sidelines. Things they typically yell include, "If you don't start throwing strikes, I will pull you from the game!" Most often, the coach and the backseat coach exchange words sometime during the game.

➤ The "criticizer" can be either a woman or a man, but most often it is a dad. This is someone who feels their little leaguer just isn't doing enough: "Get out there!" they yell, or "Get some ambition!" "Get hungry!" or

"Why are you so slow?" It's okay to scowl at the criti-cizer; everybody must show disapproval and disdain.

> The "bragger" is a parent who is constantly reminding other spectators that his or her little leaguer is better than even the best. If a compliment is given to someone else's child, the bragger will rudely interrupt, saying, "Well, you haven't seen my player, who is the fastest, the tallest, and the toughest." If the little lea-guer performed well in previous games, the parent usu-ally will announce, "So-and-so was in the zone!" Worse, the bragger will give you advice, such as, "If number nine [the bragger's little leaguer] comes into the game to pitch, then your little leaguer better get out of the way." Just roll your eyes and be patient; the bragger usually gets it in the end.

> The "socialite" usually is a mom who uses little league games to catch up on gossip, hairstyles, or shopping sprees. She usually misses the one important play that their all-star makes, and then has to ask other people who are half paying attention to the game and half paying attention to the gossip. The socialites are very distracting, as they usually have interesting informa-tion, and you can feel torn between paying attention to the ballgame or eavesdropping.

> The "nervous parent" can be found pacing behind the bleachers, sometimes smoking or chewing a stick or shoelace. Occasionally, the nervous parent can be spotted watching the game from the sidelines only to retreat to their safe place once again when the calls are becoming too close.

> The "ostrich" sits on the bleacher and hides his or her head in their lap as soon as the game gets interesting. You can recognize this person by his or her blotched face due to pressure points.

➢ The "religious person" can be found clutching rosary beads and saying, "Oh, God," "Oh, God," "What the heck?" or "Holy s—-!" Everyone will eventually do penance around this person.

➢ The "suck-ups" are parents who stand, or bring their own lawn chairs and sit, next to the dugout so they can make sure their little leaguer remains in good graces with the coach. They are always complimenting the coach: "What a great play, Coach!" "Gee, you look nice today," or "Nobody fields a game like you, Coach!"

➢ "Grunters" do not speak, cheer, or yell. They grunt and sometimes huff. Do not expect to enter into any type of conversation with a grunter.

➢ "Mumblers" comment under their breath. You might think they are talking to you, so you take your eyes off the game and look them in either the back of their head or in their eyes and say, "Huh?" Mumblers then act surprised that you are talking to them. Ignore them or change seats.

➢ The "anti-social parent" can be recognized as the one who is sitting on the top bleacher, arms folded, with a scowl on his or her face. You can't help but hate this person or persons, feeling they hate you. Sometimes this is a couple who acts aloof. Their little leaguer is better than yours or anyone else's, and they are concerned that their little leaguer is not getting the challenge or recognition they so deserve. It's very easy to plot disaster against the anti-social parents.

➢ The "talker" is someone you dread sitting near because it's like having your teeth cleaned by the dental hygienist who asks questions that require detailed answers. Mouth full of suction, moisture, blood, and sharp instruments, and they can't ask yes-and-no questions? The talker is especially annoying on days you just want to watch the game so you can discuss it with your player at home. You must not establish eye contact with the talker, so you can politely ignore the frantic waving for you to come over.

➢ The "clueless spectator" says incredibly stupid, off-the-wall remarks like "Is this the first quarter?" "Did my son make a touch down?" "Who is the point guard?" or "Where is your other glove?"

➢ The "eater" spends most of his or her game at the concession stand. The only reaction they have is to menu or candy selection changes. Certain weight gain can be expected as a result of sitting with the eater.

➢ The "downer" is the doomsday fan who doesn't see the good in anything: "This will not work," "They'll never make it," "He's going to strike out," or "She will break her leg if she slides." If the downer is a woman, she usually is worried that her little leaguer is going to get hurt or teased. You can become really depressed sitting next to the downer.

➢ The "stinker" is someone who always has terrible body odor, hasn't washed his or her hair for months, has terrible breath (and wants to talk closely), or has terrible smelling flatus. They sometimes like to sit next to the grunters, so the moans and groans mask the escaping flatus. On a warm humid day, this stink lingers and grows. You can't seem to escape it, and pretty soon it is absorbed by your clothing or food. It's only when you begin to taste it that you know for a fact the stinker is near. Always sit upwind of the stinker. If you are not sure which direction the wind is blowing, gently hold a napkin in the air and sit opposite of the way it waves.

➢ The "sunshine mom" is always cheery. She sings a soprano "Hello," smiles, and frantically waves you over, even if she doesn't know you. She always wants to hug you. She sits very close, or wants to share her bleacher pad. Even when your little leaguer strikes out, she's happy for you.

➤ The "excuse parents" are those who believe that, no matter how badly their all-star player is at baseball, it is never their childs fault for making an error, striking out, or missing an easy pop-up. Sometimes these parents begin to blame each other for their offspring's misgivings or failures. They always sit in the middle, so everybody can hear their excuses.

➤ The "academic mom" has a scholar who is playing little league baseball because he or she must for socialization purposes. This mom usually sits next to schoolteachers or administrators. It's only during her constant mathematical analysis of all plays that you recognize the academic mom.

➤ The "scrappers" are those fans who come to the game just to pick a fight. They yell loudly and always cause controversy.

➤ The "rockers" are people who rock back and forth on narrow, poorly painted, weathered bleacher benches. You find yourself having difficulty maintaining position. If you suffer from motion sickness, you'll need to stand on solid ground or take medication.

➤ The "corporate parents" are those who can't stop working during the game. Their guilt doesn't allow them to miss the game altogether, but they sit in the stands or in their cars, laptop computers on, cellular phones to their ears, totally overdressed, and occasionally waving to their little leaguer for credit. It's appropriate to scowl at this person.

Most often, experienced dads do not even venture into the bleachers—they like to hang on the fence by first or third base. By standing close to these bases, their conversation will be loud enough for the coaches to hear their unsolicited advice.

Depending on your personality, find a similarly interested fan and form a buddy system. Plan your arrivals and departures according to this system. It's usually acceptable to bring a lawn chair and sit aloof, but then you become a personality too: "the aloof." That's okay. Whether sitting by yourself or with companions, the goal is to enjoy the game and your little leaguer's participation, effort, and pride.

Chapter Nine
Outfitting your All-Star: What's the Deal with the Shoes?

Being a novice Little League Mom, you may assume that the baseball cap will be the most treasured feature of your little leaguer's baseball uniform. Some might even think the favorite item will be the uniform shirt with all the sponsors' names, team number, and color—but it's actually the shoes and how they are worn which become the status symbol of a true ball player destined for fame and success. As a good mom, you want your player to blend in with the other team members, so you and your little leaguer go to the shoe store. Oh, not the budget or discount store; no, you must go to the store where the salespeople are dressed as sports figures or officials, where a TV monitor runs continuous advertisements of famous athletes hawking the most expensive and impractical shoes, and where you sit on a hard, narrow team bench to try on shoes. Be careful that you don't sit too close to your player or it will be too obvious your player is at the mall with his or her mom.

The shoes your player typically will select from the display wall are the ones that they see on TV commercials between cartoons. You'll know these shoes are the popular ones because they cost at least one hundred dollars more than what they're worth. They have to be totally impractical, and they have to be an obnoxious color. Some pump up, some light up when players walk or run, some have holographic pictures on them that actually can make you nauseated, and some don't have laces. The only input a mom is afforded, sometimes, is asking whether they fit or not. If you're quick enough, you might be able to get in a toe squeeze.

Remember, each sport requires a special shoe. They cannot be interchanged between sports or your player will suffer irreversible psychological damage. You'll begin literally to stumble on the fact that sport shoes reproduce exponentially: baseball cleats, football cleats, golf cleats, soccer shoes or cleats, running shoes, street shoes, rollerblades, hockey skates (several types), beach shoes, boat shoes, etc. Each cleat leaves a slightly different mark on your linoleum. You'll soon learn to recognize each hole, which allows you to scold the culprit who wore cleats in the house. Players believe that their shoes will lead them to greatness. They walk onto the field, staring down at their shoes. They twist those cleats down deep into the dirt for better traction. In their minds, little leaguers can slide, kick, jump, stride, and run better because of their shoes.

Not only does your little leaguer live in these shoes, but so do other earth inhabitants, including creatures that thrive as a result of poor foot hygiene or shoe storage practices. Foot odor will be difficult to identify at first, because when it appears, it's usually a complex set of odors generated from earthworms, dog feces, gum, spit, Dad's chew, candy, and ice cream. A warning from one mom to another: Do not bring the suspect shoe up to your nose for confirmation of the stench you notice in your mudroom. The impact of the odor may cause you to stagger away or become overwhelmed by the noxious gases; you may trip over a mound of piled-high shoes and hurt yourself. Foot powder, soap, and water will assist, but a good scraping knife is your best bet. But, don't get the shoe too clean, or your player will look as if he or she doesn't play hard enough.

A true little leaguer does not commonly untie his or her baseball shoes to remove them. There is a ritual for taking off shoes. The player must engage the heel on the lip of a door jam and flick the shoe off. Sometimes if you're lucky, the shoes will hit the opposing wall hard enough to remove some of the mud, cow patties, clumps of grass, and squashed caterpillars. They then fall on the mound of other shoes, to be found during a search five minutes before game time, when panic and anxiety could lead to poor field performance.

Other than shoes, ball players also must have a batter's glove. The glove helps the batter grip the bat. When the little leaguer is not up to bat, he or she places the glove it in their back pocket with the fingers hanging out.

Now to speak of the hat: Most often, it's a team hat that matches the uniform. The player is very proud of the hat. Like the shoes, do not wash the hat. Many stores sell hat frames to help the hat maintain its shape. However, a washed hat means a bench sitter. Not good. In addition, a washed hat may shrink. If the hat doesn't fit right, then the little leaguer will become distracted, which again could lead to poor field performance for which you will be blamed. When batting, the little leaguer also must wear a batter's helmet. A batter's helmet is a requirement of all leagues. It's a kind of hard hat—very necessary for safety.

Finally, boys will eventually have to wear protective underwear, such as a jock strap and a cup. Beginning little leaguers do not know what a cup is. It's a good idea for you, the mom, to purchase the first jock strap and cup because between the dad and the son, there is no size other than extra large, no matter the age.

The only make-up that is worn is black goop painted under the players' eyes. The black goop is called "eye shadow," even though it is worn underneath, not above, the eye. In most states, little league baseball is played in the spring and summer months. Sunshine can cause a glare into a little leaguer's eyes. Eye shadow is effective in absorbing the glare. It is also a sign of a serious player.

Chapter Ten
Outfitting You, the Little League Baseball Mom

You may ask, "Well, what do I wear?" You want to fit in, and you want to look good at the same time. In my opinion and based on my extensive experience, it is more important to be comfortable. Clothes chosen for the game should be durable, and more importantly, wash-and-wear. In many cases, the ball fields can be wet, so your shoes and the bottom of your pants, legs, or the edges of a long skirt will be splashed with mud. If you sit on wooden bleachers, your nylon stockings will never survive without runs from splinters or rough, uneven edges. Metal bleachers are always cold, so if you sit on these bleachers with thin, cotton clothes, your bottom will freeze. It is more difficult to sit on bleachers with a numb, cold bottom. Sitting on bleachers with a short skirt may expose, as my mother always warned, your "business." Showing your "business" may distract male coaches and umpires enough to cause issues in the game. Climbing up bleachers, or even sitting in the first row, requires leg lifting and some twisting that you don't want to impede with a tight or floor-length skirt.

Since the game is played outdoors in a field, there are always going to be insects. Flying, crawling, nesting, buzzing, and stinging insects. Avoid clothes that will attract the insects, such as bright colors, especially florals. Also avoid excessive perfumes, as sweet odors attract insects. If using insect repellant, make sure that the repellant won't discolor your clothes.

The best outfit to wear in order to blend in with the other, more seasoned little league moms is jeans or jean shorts of a respectable length, a t-shirt (preferably a league shirt with your little leaguer's name on the back), ankle-high socks, and comfortable canvas shoes or sandles. A sun hat, or better yet, a baseball hat, can be necessary in hot weather. Remember, little league games are a great place for people-watching. Spectators at these games notice what other people are wearing; mostly women notice what other women are wearing. It is a fact of life.

Chapter Eleven
Cheering Etiquette

A major responsibility for any mom in the bleachers is to cheer for the team, but especially for her own little all-star—no matter how poorly he or she plays. This can be a tricky business, knowing what is appropriate to yell, and it will depend on the personality of the little leaguer as well as the task he or she is performing. You need to fit in. No matter how loud everyone else is yelling, cheering, and chattering, someone making an off-the-wall comment or an out-of-place cheer will deaden the crowd. So, here are some common calls and what they mean:

> ➤ "Hey, batter batter!" actually pronounced, "Hey, batta batta!" is a call of encouragement to your little leaguer who is in the batting box, warming up, and ready to swing the bat.

> ➤ "You caught them looking!" is something you can yell if your player is a pitcher. It means he or she struck someone out because the batter didn't swing, or swung the bat late.

> ➤ "Little chatter out there!" usually is called to the catcher so as to distract the batter. You can yell this when the field is silent. It means for the outfielders and

infielders to start talking, chanting, and making noise so as to distract both the batter and the base runner. It also stimulates the players. Hopefully, the chatter doesn't include things about the little leaguer's "mama." It is very uncool to scold or correct a little leaguer who is chattering in the dugout, unless, of course, the chatter contains the "F word."

➤ "Be ready!" is a nice way to yell at your little leaguer who is playing the outfield and not really paying attention. The younger the team, the more difficult it is for the outfielders to stay alert to a fly ball, which is very rare. Most often, the outfielder is laying flat on his or her back in the outfield, chasing butterflies, admiring their batting glove, or running around.

➤ "Good eye!" means that the batter didn't swing at the pitched ball because it was out of the strike zone. This phrase is used as soon as the umpire calls a ball. Some parents on the opposite team yell "Ball!" before the umpire makes the call, only to try to influence the decision. It's also good to yell "Good eye!" when the batter doesn't look like he or she even tried to hit the ball. This helps your batter save face.

➤ "Keep your head straight!" or "Where is your head pointing?" are phrases an inexperienced mom typically doesn't say. Dads usually say these things in an instructional tone when frustrated with the batter striking out while looking twisted.

➤ "Looks good to me!" is a common thing to say when the umpire, perched and looking straight at the strike zone, clearly made a mistake by calling a ball instead of a strike. This is the most important thing you can say to support a pitcher.

➤ "Swing if it's good!" is a gentle way of warning the batter that the pitcher is throwing balls. This is a cheer that is always yelled when the batter is anxious about hitting something.

➤ "Choke up!" or "Choke and poke!" means the batter should move his or her hands up toward the fat end of the bat to make contact, even if it's a foul ball. There are two strikes on the batter, and the game is close in this situation.

➤ "Swing batter!" is actually pronounced or sang, "Swwwwwing batta!" This is something you yell at the opposing batter as a power-of-suggestion attempt. The batter typically swings the bat at a pitch that looks like it's going to be called a ball.

➤ "The pitcher has a rubber arm!" is a phrase that infuriated me when my little leaguer pitched. Only cruel parents yell this at a pitcher who isn't playing well. It may anger pitchers so they start throwing strikes, or it can demean and humiliate them. (By the way, it demeans and humiliates you as well). You can only hope the pitcher throws a wild pitch and scares whoever is yelling.

➤ "He's a looker!" means that the batter is waiting to take a base on balls. This is something I have used throughout my son's little league, high school, junior college, and university pitching experiences. It is not meant to insult the batter, only to tempt the batter to hit the next pitched ball. It is most effective during a full count.

➤ "Down in the dirt!" encourages the runner to slide into the base, as the ball is being thrown in for an out. This is usually yelled with great enthusiasm because it's a close play. Unfortunately, little brothers and sisters hear the yell and gladly oblige.

➤ "You're alright!" or "Walk it off!" are what a mom yells when her little leaguer is only slightly hurt on the field. Depending on the age, the little leaguer cries or wants to sit on the bench as soon as any pain is experienced. It will take some practice to know when your child truly is okay or when he or she has compound tibia fracture.

➢ "Walk is as good as a hit!" is something you say when your little leaguer has just watched three balls pass by and is getting ready to swing at the next pitch.

➢ "Tighten up the defense now!" means your team just dropped the ball, missed a play, or somehow missed the out.

➢ "Good effort!" means that the batter hit the ball and almost made it to a base before getting out.

➢ "Brush 'em back!" encourages the pitcher to pitch the ball to push the batter who is crowding the plate. There is no control for a pitcher in this stage of their career, though, so "Brush 'em back!" usually means the batter is going to get beaned by the ball.

These are the commonly accepted cheers, but remember, you never know whether little leaguers can or cannot hear you when they are out on the playing field. Be careful not to be mean-spirited, as this could shape a future Jeffrey Dahmer or Charles Manson.

Chapter Twelve
Sitting the Bench: When the Coach Doesn't Play Your Baby

No one really prepares you for watching your little leaguer humiliated while he or she sits on the bench with legs spread, hands wringing, head hanging, waiting for the moment the coach will tap him or her on the shoulder and say, "You're up." When the moment comes, however, there usually is only one inning left in the game. Your all-star plays hard in the last few minutes of the game, even though he or she is cold and stiff from sitting the bench.

As you surge with helplessness and despair, pulsating with vengeance, the thoughts that will go through your mind are not pleasant. You will find yourself glaring not only at the coach, but also at the parents whose little leaguer is getting great playing time. You can't help but hate everybody. The game is over; you must wait for your little leaguer to come out of the dugout. You hope he or she is not emotionally scarred from other kids mocking them for sitting on the bench. This is where self-restraint becomes very important. Do not cry! As you are waiting, it's not uncommon to run into the coach. You will begin to glare as you see him or her. Your heart will race, you will feel an urgency to void, your stomach will be sick, and you will have an incredible urge to say something. You will begin making mental death wishes against this coach. You will want so much to hug your little leaguer, your baby—but do not pity your child. Typical reasons why a coach doesn't award playing time to a little leaguer include not showing up for practice, poor attitude, poor grades, and politics.

Do not ask your player, "So, why do you think you're not getting playing time?"

Do not criticize any lack of talent: "Move your feet;" "You're too slow;" "Are you working hard enough?" Don't say things like, "Well, I see so-and-so practicing every day; how come you're not?" Don't compare your player to someone else. Do not send death wishes or threats to the coach. Finally, be prepared for the coach's vengeance when you complain to him or her. Coaches think they are right and can't be questioned.

Chapter Thirteen
When Your Husband Is the Coach, You Are the First Lady

When you are married to the coach, you are expected to assume the role of Mrs. Coach. You are supposed to know as much as your husband does about his team. This also means you're responsible for the decisions your husband makes, as well as who he plays in which positions, what plays he calls, how much playing time is awarded, uniform numbers, whether the stirrups match the jersey, sponsors, and even rainouts. You also are expected to do a lot more for the league than anyone else. You and your husband arrive at the games together, which can be okay, but the trunk is full of dirty, dusty equipment such as bags with clamoring bats, balls, umpire's chest protectors, clipboards with batting rosters, a huge water cooler, and a first aid kit. Try to get out of the car fast enough to avoid the unloading process, as there usually are no hand washing facilities in the portable bathrooms.

You always will be responsible for providing water, first aid, and paperwork. It is not uncommon to see the coach leaning over the dugout fence to say, "Honey, have you seen my batting roster?" or "Honey, can you go home and get…" People will approach you and provide vacation times, etc. Then there is the dreaded "stats keeper" role, which you may have to assume. You also may be responsible for laundering uniforms after the season is over.

The worst job delegated to you, the First Lady, is that of team photographer. No matter what the age of the team, the coach likes a tape of the game for analysis and critique. This is a particularly difficult job because you have to stand close to the action, which requires a certain alertness. Getting hit by a fly ball not only hurts and leaves a mark, but also is embarrassing, especially when your husband ignores your bloody head wound and your little leaguers are embarrassed that you had the audacity to get hit. Keeping the camera steady is not as easy as it looks. When the tape is viewed, it is very frustrating to hear all the screaming and cheering, and to see only dirt, grass, or chalk lines. This occurs when you turn your head to watch the game with your own eyes instead of through the video camera. Even if you are watching younger siblings, the first priority is to get that recording. These tapes become priceless treasures in years to follow.

Chapter Fourteen
When You Have to Speak Out

There will be times when you can't ignore a situation, and you must speak out. It will take practice learning just when it is appropriate. Here are some case studies to assist you in your learning process.

When the weather is hot, sunny, and humid almost to the point of being unbearable, the team enjoys a cold glass of water, a pop, or a popsicle at the end of the game. If coaches choose to punish the team because of losing or because of botched plays, and they take the beverage away, this is one of those times you must speak up loud and clear.

When the coach is humiliating a player—"You are never going to play the infield because you are slow or stupid," or "You just don't have it" (talking to a seven-year-old)—it's time to get up and give the coach the "lioness protecting her cub" look. Learn to give an intimidating look. It works.

Sometimes you have to speak out to the local law enforcement. Many a time, as a seasoned Little League Mom, I have had to call 911 to report threats against either team members (even as young as eight years old) or the umpires. You tend to hear these threats in the bleachers. First it may be said as an innocent remark to the next person: "I think I may wait for that coach after the game and teach them the league rules," or "I am going to find out what car that umpire is driving." It can get really bad when the disgruntled spectator makes threats to the umpire during the game.

A coach may have to speak out to the local press when a little leaguer's parent is trying to bring a law suit against the coach because of playing time.

Chapter Fifteen
The All-Star Game

A t the end of the season, there typically is an All-star game
for those little leaguers who are selected, usually by their
teammates, to represent the team. Depending on the league, two
or three players will go to the all-star game. The election process
can create serious problems for the family. For example, if you
have two little leaguers playing in the same league, and one gets
picked and the other does not, or if your little leaguer's friends are
all picked for teams, and your little leaguer is not among them—
be prepared to comfort your child, as there is rarely anything you
can do—unless the coach is a relative, of course.

Most often, the volunteer coach picks his or her own son or
daughter, regardless of talent, even if the coach has to change the
team's vote. The coach figures having an "all-star" in the family
is payback for their time and effort. Being chosen is not about
talent, but often who you know.

The all-star game is all about bragging rights. Just like pro-
fessional baseball, in little league there is big fame associated with
being an all-star player. Based on league finances, the all-star
players will be outfitted with a special jersey or hat. All-star
players strut their stuff wearing their new gear. Being an all-star
player earns the player certain considerations for the next season.

Be careful that if you become an all star player's mother, you do not become "the bragger." Fellow league participants loathe "the bragger."

Chapter Sixteen
The Grand Finale

The season usually concludes with a picnic or some other gathering where trophies are awarded, uniforms are turned in, and farewells can be forwarded properly. There is a certain resolution to the grand finale. You get to say goodbye. However, the grand finale means a lot of work for the Little League Mom. You might have to bring a dish to pass at a picnic. Don't forget to turn in a washed uniform, if required.

It is a good idea to give a gift or card to the coach as a show of appreciation for his or her hard work and dedication. Shake the coach's hand, as he or she has volunteered a lot of time and become a part of your little leaguer's childhood memories. This gesture of appreciation is important, even if you didn't like the coach's style. If your little leaguer desires to play sports in the future, you never know when you could run into this coach again.

At high school graduation parties, my husband (a long-time little league coach) received thank you cards from past little leaguers who addressed the cards, "To my first baseball family." Little things in life matter. Little league baseball is part of it.

Take pictures, and hang them on your "hall of fame" wall. Arrange the pictures by year or season so you can watch all the players grow up. You will catch yourself looking at these pictures through the years and thinking, "She was right—it was the best time of my life."

Enjoy every minute of little league.

Play Ball!